Map It!™

CLIMATE MAPS

Ian F. Mahaney

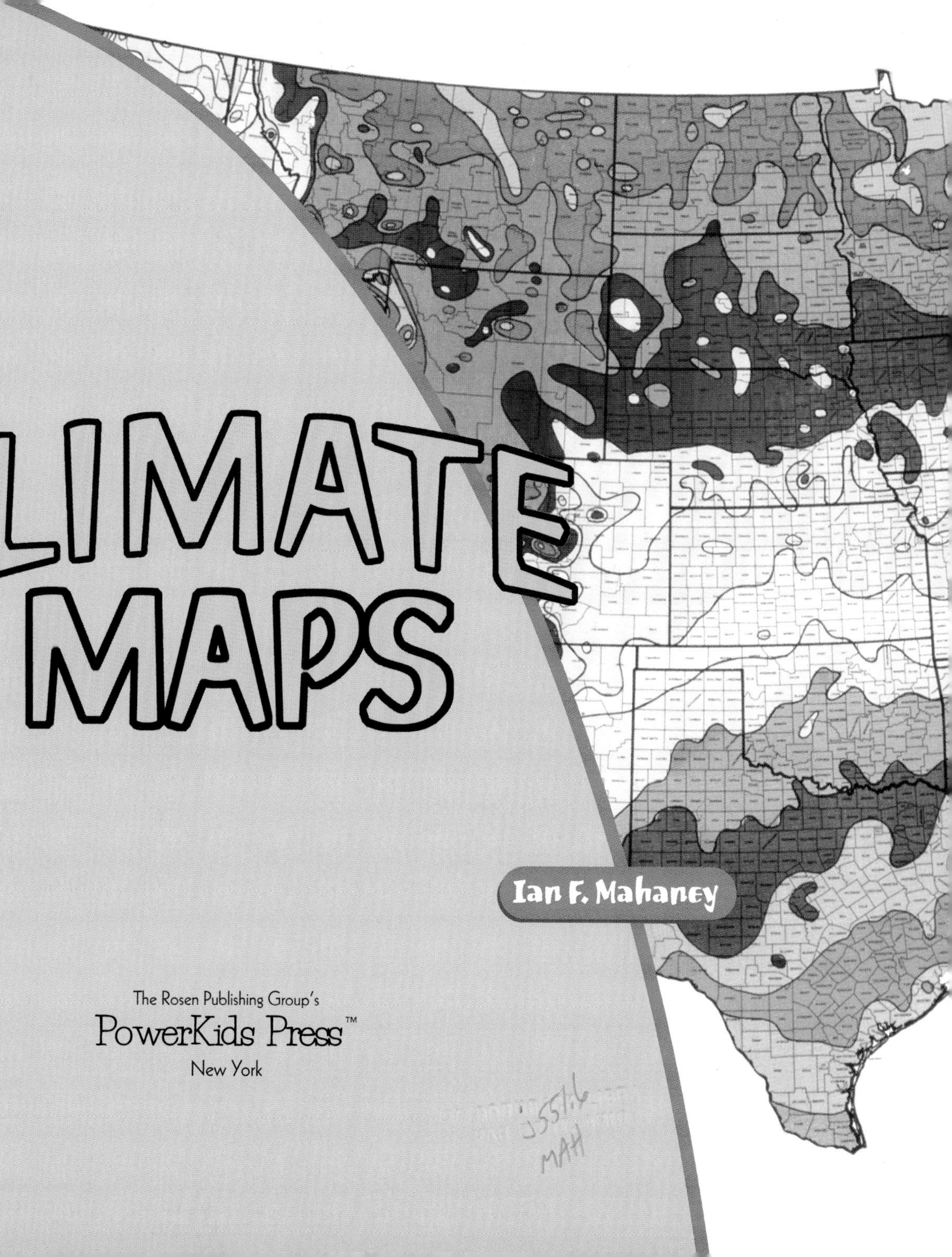

The Rosen Publishing Group's

PowerKids Press™

New York

To my parents, who still deal with me daily

Published in 2007 by The Rosen Publishing Group, Inc.
29 East 21st Street, New York, NY 10010

First Edition

Editor: Jennifer Way
Designer: Greg Tucker
Photo Researcher: Jeffrey Wendt

Photo Credits: Cover, pp. 1, 21 Agricultural Research Service, USDA; cover (left) © Royalty-Free/Corbis; pp. 5, 10, 14, 18 © 2004, Spatial Climate Analysis Service, Oregon State University; pp. 6, 9, Library of Congress Geography and Map Division; 13 (top), 17 Western Regional Climate Center, Desert Research Institute and Spatial Climate Analysis Service, Oregon State University, p. 13 (bottom) JPL/NASA.

Library of Congress Cataloging-in-Publication Data

Mahaney, Ian F.
  Climate maps / Ian F. Mahaney.— 1st ed.
      p. cm. — (Map it!)
  Includes bibliographical references and index.
  ISBN 1-4042-3058-0 (lib. bdg.) — ISBN 1-4042-2214-6 (pbk.) — ISBN 1-4042-2404-1 (six pack)
  1. Map reading—Juvenile literature. 2. Climatology—Juvenile literature. I. Title. II. Series.

  GA130.M357 2007
  551.6022'3—dc22

                                    2005033442

Manufactured in the United States of America

Contents

Maps are some of the most useful things ever created. Maps are **representations** of places. There are many types of maps that can tell us different kinds of **information** about the area they show. Some maps can show the natural features of an area, such as rivers, mountains, and deserts. Other maps may show humanmade features, such as cities, roads, and borders. Maps can show towns, states, countries, or even the whole world.

Most maps have a few things in common. Maps show information using **symbols**. The **legend** on a map will explain these symbols to you. Maps also use a **compass rose** to explain the four main directions, which are north, south, east, and west. This book will teach you how to read and understand **climate** maps.

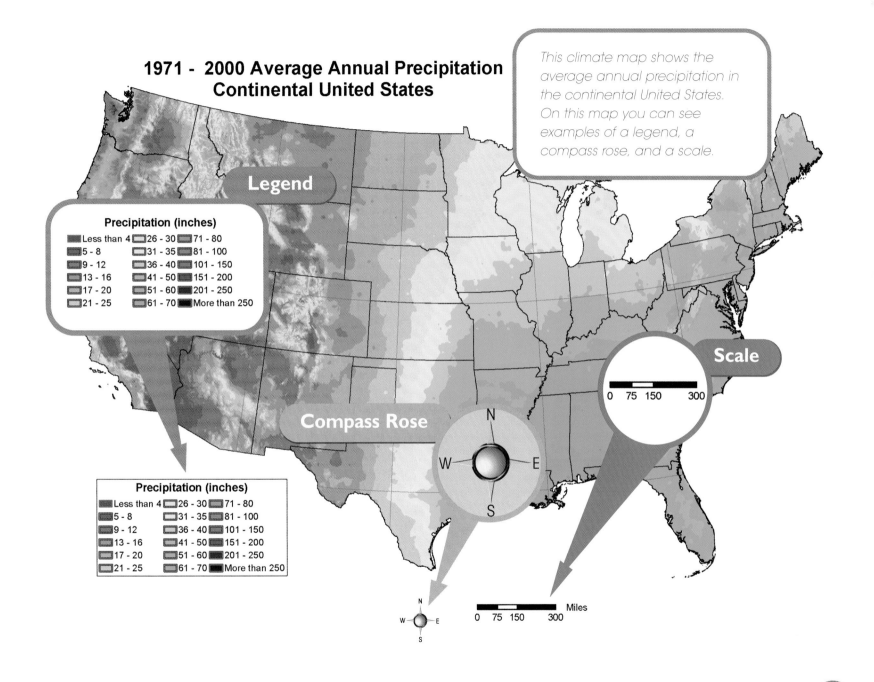

1971 - 2000 Average Annual Precipitation Continental United States

This climate map shows the average annual precipitation in the continental United States. On this map you can see examples of a legend, a compass rose, and a scale.

Legend

Precipitation (inches)

Less than 4	26 - 30	71 - 80
5 - 8	31 - 35	81 - 100
9 - 12	36 - 40	101 - 150
13 - 16	41 - 50	151 - 200
17 - 20	51 - 60	201 - 250
21 - 25	61 - 70	More than 250

Precipitation (inches)

Less than 4	26 - 30	71 - 80
5 - 8	31 - 35	81 - 100
9 - 12	36 - 40	101 - 150
13 - 16	41 - 50	151 - 200
17 - 20	51 - 60	201 - 250
21 - 25	61 - 70	More than 250

Compass Rose

N
W E
S

Scale

0 75 150   300

N
W E
S

0 75 150   300   Miles

5

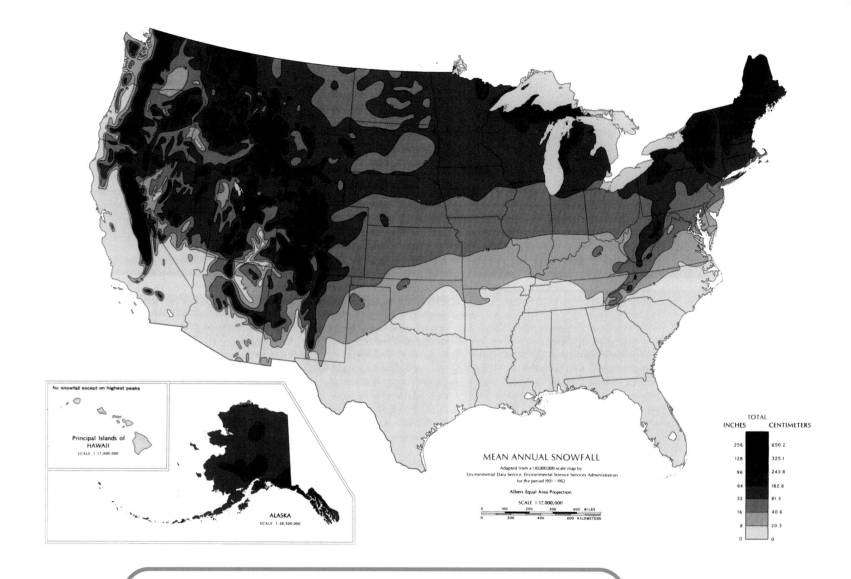

MEAN ANNUAL SNOWFALL

Adapted from a 1:10,000,000-scale map by
Environmental Data Service, Environmental Science Services Administration
for the period 1931 – 1952

Albers Equal Area Projection

SCALE 1:17,000,000

| 0 | 100 | 200 | 300 | 400 | MILES |

| 0 | 200 | 400 | 600 | KILOMETERS |

No snowfall except on highest peaks

Principal Islands of
HAWAII
SCALE 1:17,000,000

ALASKA
SCALE 1:38,500,000

TOTAL	
INCHES	CENTIMETERS
256	650.2
128	325.1
96	243.8
64	162.6
32	81.3
16	40.6
8	20.3
0	0

*This climate map shows the mean yearly snowfall in the United States.
The mean is the average amount. To make this map, people who
study climate measured the total amounts of snow that fell each year.
After they collected the information for many years, they could figure
out the average.*

What Is Climate?

Have you ever watched a weather report and wondered where weather comes from? Weather is created by a mix of heat, **air pressure**, wind, and moisture in the **atmosphere**. How are weather and climate related? When people talk about the weather, they usually mean the conditions in the short term. This means what will happen the next day or the next week. When people talk about the average weather of an area over a longer period of time, they are talking about the climate.

The climate of an area tells us what the average weather has been like. This can help us forecast the weather, or figure out what kind of weather to expect. For example, if the average yearly snowfall in Minnesota is about 32 inches (81 cm), we can expect it to snow about that much each year there.

A climate map shows the climate for an area. Climate maps usually show one type of weather condition. This helps you understand how that type of weather has an effect on an area. For example, a climate map might show the amount of **precipitation** that an area gets. Precipitation is any moisture that falls from the clouds. Rain, snow, and sleet are all types of precipitation. Other climate maps might show the **temperature** of an area. Temperature maps and precipitation maps are two of the most common kinds of climate maps. Climate maps can show other weather features, such as wind speed, sunshine, or **humidity**. You can find out what kinds of weather are represented on a climate map by looking at the legend.

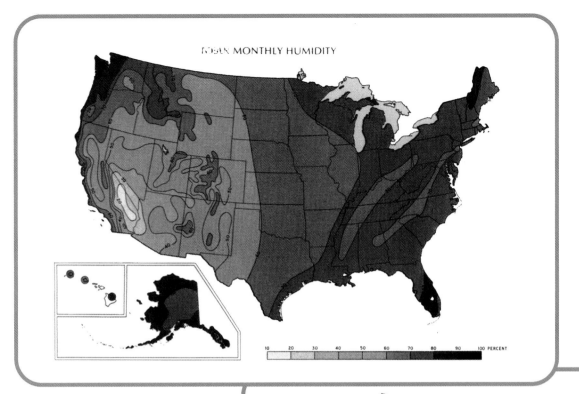

MEAN MONTHLY HUMIDITY

10 20 30 40 50 60 70 80 90 100 PERCENT

Climate maps can be made for many different weather conditions. The map on the top shows the average humidity in October across the United States. The map on the bottom shows the average number of sunny days in October across the United States. The legends on these maps help you read the information about humidity and the number of sunny days.

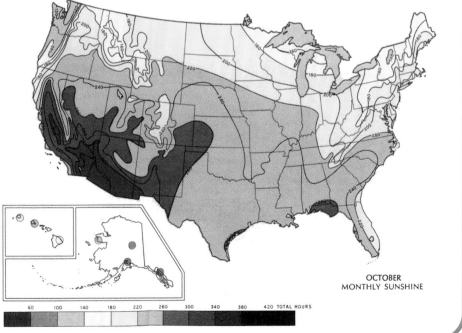

OCTOBER
MONTHLY SUNSHINE

60 100 140 180 220 260 300 340 380 420 TOTAL HOURS

1971 - 2000 Average July Temperature

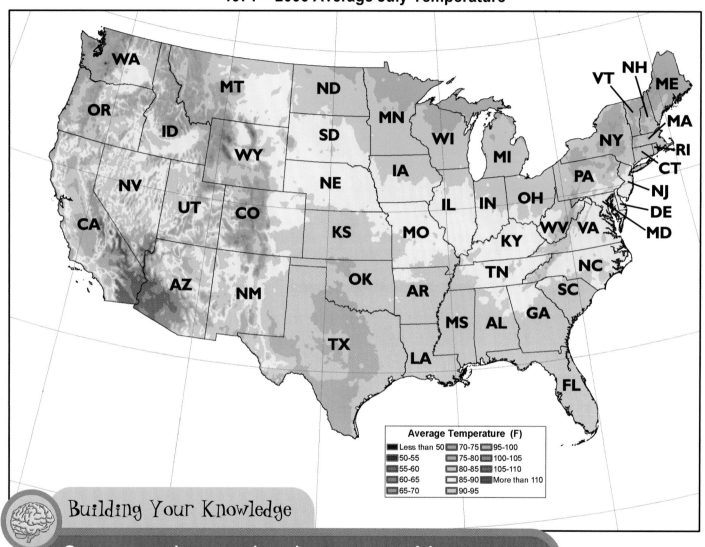

Average Temperature (F)

Less than 50	70-75	95-100
50-55	75-80	100-105
55-60	80-85	105-110
60-65	85-90	More than 110
65-70	90-95	

Building Your Knowledge

Can you name the states where there are average July temperatures of over 100° F (38° C)? The answer is below.

Answer: California, Arizona, Nevada, Utah, New Mexico, Texas, Kansas, and Oklahoma.

The Legend

It is important to understand the symbols used on a map's legend. On a climate map, the legend explains the colors and symbols used on the map. Look at the climate map on the left. It shows the average July temperatures across the United States. Can you find the legend?

On a climate map, temperature is usually shown with colors. The legend will tell you what these colors represent. For example, red usually stands for warmer weather. Blue stands for cooler weather. On this map the legend tells you that dark orange or red represents an average July temperature that is greater than 100° F (38° C). See if you can find the average July temperature of Maine.

Latitude and Climate

On a map of the world, you will see a **latitude** line called the **equator**. The equator separates Earth into the Northern **Hemisphere** and the Southern Hemisphere. The areas near the equator are the warmest in the world. The North Pole and the South Pole are the farthest from the equator. They are usually the coldest parts of Earth.

The amount of sunlight an area receives has an effect on its climate. Earth turns on its **axis** once each day, which is why there is day and night. The Earth also circles the Sun once each year. The Earth's axis is **tilted**. As Earth circles the Sun, different areas get different amounts and strengths of sunlight. This is why there are seasons. You can see the effect the seasons have on climate if you look at climate maps of the same area from different times of the year.

California Average August Precipitation

California Average January Precipitation

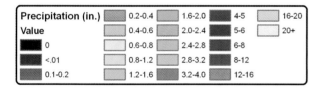

Precipitation (in.) Value			
0	0.2-0.4	1.6-2.0	4-5	16-20
<.01	0.4-0.6	2.0-2.4	5-6	20+
0.1-0.2	0.6-0.8	2.4-2.8	6-8	
	0.8-1.2	2.8-3.2	8-12	
	1.2-1.6	3.2-4.0	12-16	

Building Your Knowledge

Because Earth's axis is tilted, the strength and amount of sunlight received by areas of the world changes throughout the year. The difference is greater the farther north or south in latitude you go. When the sunlight is weaker and lasts fewer hours, it is winter. When the sunlight is stronger and lasts longer, it is summer. Areas near the equator get about the same amount and strength of sunlight throughout the year. The climate stays about the same year-round.

By looking at climate maps of the same area from different times of the year, you can see how the seasons have an effect on the weather. Compare these two precipitation maps of California. You can see that it is much drier in August than it is in January.

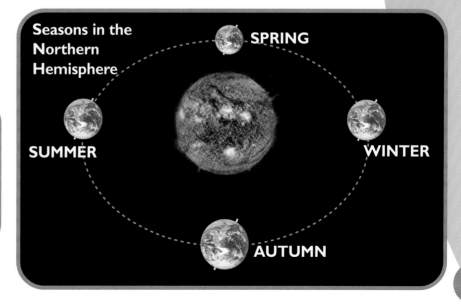

Seasons in the Northern Hemisphere

SPRING

SUMMER

WINTER

AUTUMN

1971 - 2000 Average Maximum Temperature
July, New Jersey

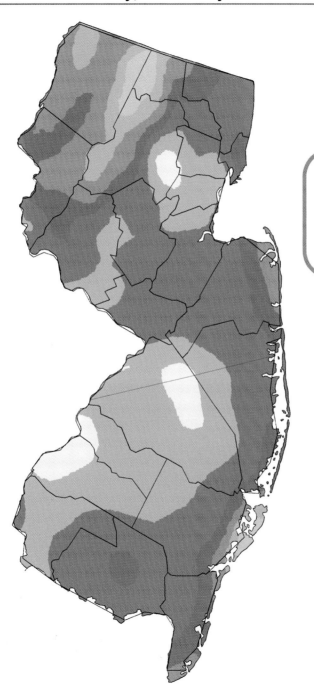

This map shows New Jersey's average July maximum, or high, temperature. This information was gathered over 30 years.

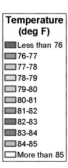

Temperature (deg F)

- Less than 76
- 76-77
- 77-78
- 78-79
- 79-80
- 80-81
- 81-82
- 82-83
- 83-84
- 84-85
- More than 85

Temperature Maps and Precipitation Maps

Temperature climate maps tell us how warm or cool an area usually is. This type of temperature map can look at the average temperature for a year. Temperature maps can also show a certain time of year, such as a season or a month. The map on the left shows the average July temperature in New Jersey. Its legend shows the different temperature ranges in New Jersey.

A precipitation map shows how much and what kind of precipitation is common in an area. Precipitation maps can show the average amount of one type of precipitation. They can also show the average amount of precipitation for a season or a month or the average number of days of precipitation per year.

Scientists classify, or group, climates into five major climate **zones**. These zones classify climates by average temperature and precipitation. They are **tropical**, dry, **temperate**, cold, and **polar**.

A tropical climate, such as that in Hawaii, is warm and wet. A dry climate, such as that in Arizona, does not get much rain and is usually warm. A temperate climate, such as that in Ohio, has warm summers and mild winters. A cold climate, such as that in Alaska, has warm summers and cold winters. Polar climates are cold year-round and can be found in the areas around the North Pole and the South Pole. The climates are further sorted by the amount of precipitation and other weather conditions. Look at the map on the left. Which climate zone do you live in?

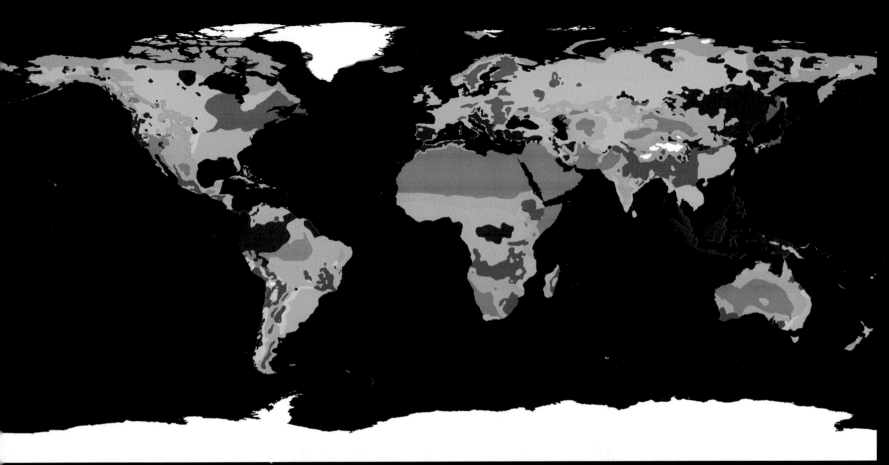

Koeppen's Climate Classification

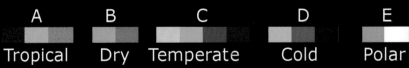

A	B	C	D	E
Tropical	Dry	Temperate	Cold	Polar

This map of the world shows the five major climate zones. You can see that there are smaller groupings within some of these climate zones. These smaller groupings show how much precipitation different areas get.

WASHINGTON
Average Annual Precipitation

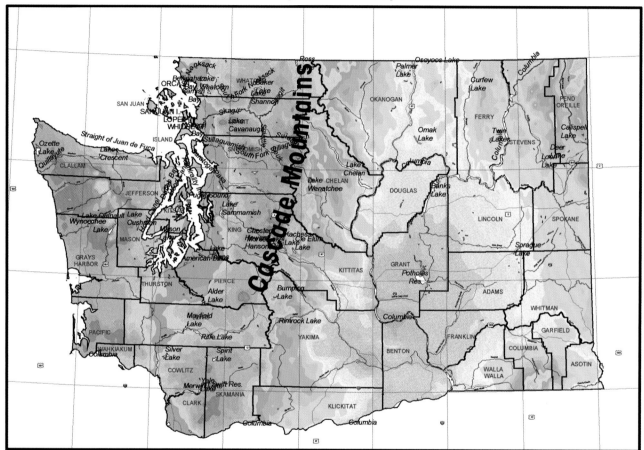

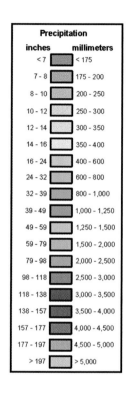

Precipitation	
inches	**millimeters**
< 7	< 175
7 - 8	175 - 200
8 - 10	200 - 250
10 - 12	250 - 300
12 - 14	300 - 350
14 - 16	350 - 400
16 - 24	400 - 600
24 - 32	600 - 800
32 - 39	800 - 1,000
39 - 49	1,000 - 1,250
49 - 59	1,250 - 1,500
59 - 79	1,500 - 2,000
79 - 98	2,000 - 2,500
98 - 118	2,500 - 3,000
118 - 138	3,000 - 3,500
138 - 157	3,500 - 4,000
157 - 177	4,000 - 4,500
177 - 197	4,500 - 5,000
> 197	> 5,000

On this precipitation map of Washington, you can see that the average yearly precipitation is much higher in the western part of the state than in the eastern part of the state. One reason that there are two microclimates in the state is because the Cascade Mountains separate the state into two parts.

Microclimates

A climate map usually looks at a large area. We can also look at the climate of a smaller area, or a microclimate. When you look at a map that shows microclimates, you can see where the climate changes a lot between two neighboring areas. Many natural features, such as mountains and oceans, can have an effect on the climate.

For example, the state of Washington has one of the highest average yearly precipitation amounts in the United States. Look at a map that shows the state's microclimates. It rains much more in the state's western part than it does in the eastern part. That is because the Cascade Mountains separate the state into two parts. Rain clouds come off the Pacific Ocean and travel over the state. The mountains act as a wall that keeps the clouds from crossing over to the eastern part of the state.

Everyday Uses for Climate Maps

Gardeners often use climate maps. Plants depend on having a certain kind of weather to grow. A gardener can use a climate map to see if where he or she lives has the right weather for certain plants to grow. A climate map will show, based on location, what time of year is the best time to plant certain seeds.

Look at the plant hardiness map shown here. It shows the average date of the last **frost** in the spring. The companies that sell seeds use maps like these to advise gardeners of the best time to plant seeds based on where they live. A gardener who lives in Montana would need to plant her tomatoes later in the spring than would a gardener who lives in Tennessee. Can you think of crops that are more successful in certain areas because the climate is right for them there?

AVERAGE ANNUAL MINIMUM TEMPERATURE

Temperature (°C)	Zone	Temperature (°F)
-45.6 and Below	1	Below -50
-42.8 to -45.5	2a	-45 to -50
-40.0 to -42.7	2b	-40 to -45
-37.3 to -40.0	3a	-35 to -40
-34.5 to -37.2	3b	-30 to -35
-31.7 to -34.4	4a	-25 to -30
-28.9 to -31.6	4b	-20 to -25
-26.2 to -28.8	5a	-15 to -20
-23.4 to -26.1	5b	-10 to -15
-20.6 to -23.3	6a	-5 to -10
-17.8 to -20.5	6b	0 to -5
-15.0 to -17.7	7a	5 to 0
-12.3 to -15.0	7b	10 to 5
-9.5 to -12.2	8a	15 to 10
-6.7 to -9.4	8b	20 to 15
-3.9 to -6.6	9a	25 to 20
-1.2 to -3.8	9b	30 to 25
1.6 to -1.1	10a	35 to 30
4.4 to 1.7	10b	40 to 35
4.5 and Above	11	40 and Above

Building Your Knowledge

Imagine that you want to plant tomatoes in your backyard. Look at the map. When would be the best time for you to start planting your tomato garden where you live?

21

Earth's average temperatures have changed throughout history. Climate change is natural. There have been periods called ice ages when the climate has been colder. There have also been periods when Earth's climate has gotten warmer. Have you ever heard people talk about global warming? This means that Earth has been getting warmer at a faster pace than it has at other times in history. Warmer temperatures may create more storms. Warmer temperatures also melt ice at the poles.

Scientists have many different theories, or ideas, to explain global warming. Some think it is a natural climate change. Most believe that pollution is one cause of the increased speed of climate change. Scientists say that it is important to make changes that might help slow climate change. No matter what causes climate change, scientists will use climate maps to help keep track of Earth's weather.

Glossary

air pressure (EHR PREH-shur) The weight of the air.

atmosphere (AT-muh-sfeer) The gases around an object in space.

axis (AK-sus) A straight line on which an object turns or seems to turn.

climate (KLY-mit) Having to do with the kind of weather a certain area has.

compass rose (KUM-pus ROHZ) A drawing on a map that shows directions.

equator (ih-KWAY-tur) An imaginary line around Earth that separates it into two parts, northern and southern.

frost (FROST) A thin covering of ice that settles on the ground on cold nights.

hemisphere (HEH-muh-sfeer) One half of Earth or another sphere.

humidity (hyoo-MIH-dih-tee) The amount of moisture in the air.

information (in-fer-MAY-shun) Knowledge or facts.

latitude (LA-tih-tood) The distance north or south of the equator.

legend (LEH-jend) A box on a map that tells what the figures on the map mean.

polar (POH-lur) Having to do with the areas around the North Pole and the South Pole.

precipitation (preh-sih-pih-TAY-shun) Any moisture that falls from the sky.

representations (reh-prih-zen-TAY-shunz) Things that stand for other things.

symbols (SIM-bulz) Objects or pictures that stand for something else.

temperate (TEM-puh-rit) Not too hot or too cold.

temperature (TEM-pur-cher) How hot or cold something is.

tilted (TILT-ed) Raised or tipped into a sloped or angled position.

tropical (TRAH-puh-kul) Warm year-round.

zones (ZOHNZ) Large areas.

Index

Web Sites

Due to the changing nature of Internet links, PowerKids Press has developed an online list of Web sites related to the subject of this book. This site is updated regularly. Please use this link to access the list:

www.powerkidslinks.com/mapit/climate/